# Epic Journeys
## coloring book

ILLUSTRATIONS BY JEFF EASLEY · LARRY ELMORE · DANA KNUTSON · MARK A. NELSON

**Kalmbach Books**
21027 Crossroads Circle
Waukesha, Wisconsin 53186

**© 2016 Kalmbach Books**
**Cover illustration: Jeff Easley**

**ISBN:** 978-1-62700-430-5

Manufactured in China.
20 19 18 17 16     1 2 3 4 5

Library of Congress Control Number:  2016943698

# The Epic Journeys

# Jeff Easley

Jeff was born in Nicholasville, Kentucky, in 1954. He showed an early interest in art, especially when it had a fantastic element, and he is a huge Frank Frazetta fan.

After graduating from Murray State University in 1977, he had a brief fling at freelancing that resulted in projects with Warren Publishing (publisher of *Vampirella* and *Creepy*) and Marvel Comics.

In 1982, he joined TSR, which was known for its Dungeons & Dragons role-playing game. During his 20+ year tenure at TSR/Wizards of the Coast, Jeff illustrated many covers for products found in TSR's gaming worlds. He was also responsible for many famous Dragonlance and Drizzt paintings.

After parting ways with WOTC in 2003, Jeff began freelancing once again, and he currently is producing art for various companies and individuals.

# Aurora's Fairyland Odyssey

When Aurora left her house that warm spring morning,
she felt it might be an unusual day. She didn't know
how unusual until she happened across a hatching
dragon egg!

As everyone knows, a dragon hatchling grants a wish to the first person it sees. Aurora knew exactly what her wish would be. She always wanted to visit every realm where fairyfolk dwelled. And their first stop was the fairy glade in the nearby forest.

The next stop was deep under the sea for an audience
with the Queen of the Mermaids. Aurora was surprised
how easy it was to breathe seawater when she had
a magic dragon as a traveling companion. In another
stroke of luck, it just happened to be bath day!

Quickly traveling to the other side of the world, she met
an enormous genie who was thrilled to reduce the
clutter in his treasure cave by giving her a huge ruby as
a souvenir.

On the high plains beyond the Mystic Mountains, Aurora watched the elven riders display their horsemanship skills. Aurora waved at the Captain of the Guard, and he waved back!

The last leg of her journey was the longest as Aurora
joined the moon sprites for tea. Although they offered
her tasty cookies, she dared not spoil her dinner. At
journey's end, she parted ways with her dragon friend
and thanked him for giving her an adventure she would
never forget!

# Mark A. Nelson

Mark has taught art at Northern Illinois University, was department head in Animation at Madison Area Technical College, and taught sequential art at Savannah College of Art and Design. He was also an art director at Pi Studios and a senior artist at Raven Software. Some of the games he worked on are Star Wars: Jedi Knights, Star Trek: Elite Force, Soldier of Fortune, and Doom.

In addition to fully painted artwork, Mark uses a range of media including pencils, pen and ink, and digital techniques. His work has appeared on products for FASA, Five Rings Publishing, Paizo Publishing, TSR, World of Warcraft, and Wizards of the Coast.

He has also drawn comics for Dark Horse, DC, Eclipse, First Comics, Kitchen Sink, Marvel, and others.

Mark is currently a freelance artist at Grazing Dinosaur Press, where he works on a variety of projects.

# Happy Trails

Every fortnight, Wizard Wally, Hazel the Badger, and
Chirp the Raven journey to the castle. Their first stop is
to hear the newest orchestrations by Duke Pleco and his
Forest Notes.

The second league of their trek brings them to Sigg's
Ibexuffalo farm, where Hazel must feed her favorite,
aHic Bee, and any others who come to the fence.

Luncheon is most often taken at Stan's roadside
food stand. Hazel always inquires about the special
ingredients, and Chirp usually partakes of the
suet special.

The afternoon finds them crossing the Troll Bridge,
where the troll family starts to waken and stir about as
their day begins.

Just outside the castle, they stop to watch Professor
Jef-fe's puppet show, which is full of heroic characters,
monsters, history, and fun. A favorite of all—full of lively
entertainment and never a blank stage.

When the travelers finally arrive at the castle, they
always meet an interesting mix of creatures, and a new
adventure begins!

# Larry Elmore

Larry started doing fantasy art when he was in college during the 1960s. Back then, none of his instructors knew what kind of "stuff" he was painting! In 1978, as a freelancer, Larry started doing paintings and drawings for *National Lampoon* and *Heavy Metal* magazines.

In 1981, he became a full-time artist for TSR, where he worked until 1987. During his years there, he did cover paintings for Dungeons & Dragons and other fantasy gaming products.

Since 1987, Larry has established himself as a successful freelance artist. He has completed artwork for various companies, including DC Comics, Eclipse Comics, FASA, Lucas Films, Game Designers' Workshop, Iron Crown, Mayfair Games, White Wolf Publishing, and Wizards of the Coast.

Larry paints the old-fashioned way, by hand, with brushes and oil paint. He draws with pencils and pens…and loves it!

# Evonna the Enchantress

Evonna loved her life as a Caretaker of Hearthwood
Deep, a great, ancient forest. One beautiful, sunny
day, the Keeper, the mysterious ruler of all Caretakers,
summoned her to his home, so Evonna set off on her
journey to the very center of Hearthwood Deep.

When the trees became so large that they blocked the sunlight, Evonna knew she was close to the Keeper's house. The door swung open at her touch, and she walked reverently to his throne. An Ancient One— covered in fur, scales, feathers and horns. He placed his hand lightly on her head, and she could feel magical power surge through her.

The Keeper told her he wanted her to take his place,
"Evonna the Enchantress, you will be ruler of all the
Caretakers." He also told her that she would have
three magical dreams that would teach her more
about Hearthwood Deep. The first dream was about all
creatures that flew.

Hearthwood Deep has many rivers, and in the second dream, Evonna was underwater, but she had changed into a mermaid! Evonna was fascinated by all that surrounded her including creatures such as alligators and turtles and frogs and fish. A complete new world unveiled itself to her as she swam down deeper into the water.

In her third dream, it was night, and the moon and stars shone brightly. Evonna floated through the forest, even down into the ground, where streams of light flowed like rivers. She saw all the animals and insects that lived in underground dens, burrows, or holes. Through her dreams, she had learned that Hearthwood Deep was a beautiful and magical place!

It was then time for the Keeper to leave, and the home
became Evonna's. The house began to change, even
the throne, to reflect Evonna's spirit. It now had a warm
and comfortable feel. An old wolf, raven, and owl joined
her. Evonna sat on her throne, thinking about the many
challenges that lay ahead in making Hearthwood Deep a
more enchanted forest.

# Dana Knutson

Dana began painting and drawing at an early age—whatever he could imagine. He feels very lucky to have grown up in a family that tolerated his interests in the bizarre and the fantastic.

After a brief tour of duty in the military, he studied art at the Malaysian Institute of Art in Kuala Lumpur, before graduating from the University of Wisconsin Stevens Point.

His first professional job was as an artist at FASA, and a decade later, he became an illustrator at TSR. There, as a concept artist, he brought the Planescape world to life along with creating it's main character, the Lady of Pain, one of his favorite projects.

Dana lives in Seattle with his wife Dawn and their cat, and he continues to do fantasy art, primarily in the video game industry.

# Return of the Queen

Much time had passed since Arlana began her travels
to distant lands. Now, she was returning to the place
where her heart had always been. Arlana looked out her
magical coach at the enchanted surroundings.

Arlana stepped from the coach and stopped to gaze
upon the great door of the castle and its symbolic feline
crest. Her heart soared as she walked slowly along the
familiar pathway.

Passing through the courtyard, the eyes of the cat-god statue seemed to follow Arlana as she continued on to the royal chamber, where she had played as a young girl.

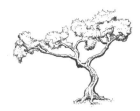

She paused momentarily at the ancient, grand marble
staircase, which was inlaid with a fanciful seascape,
before moving purposefully toward her destiny under
the watchful gaze of the exalted dragon.

Arlana's future was then realized when she was crowned as Queen of All Cats before many of her subjects. She promised to be an understanding ruler, using much of the wisdom she acquired on her recent journeys.

As she settled into her new role as queen, Arlana
recognized another truth: that happiness is being home
among your friends.

# Color Palette

# Color Palette

# How to Manage a

# MAMMOTH

A book for children and families living with **type 1 diabetes**

# This is Me

I am **Jake**.
I am 8. I go to Castle primary school.
My teacher is Mr Williams.

The most important things to me are: **football**, **building cool stuff**, my **friends** and my **mum**.

# This is Mum

Mum is **Rachel**. Mum is 35.

Mum works in an office. It's very boring but she gets to sit in a spinny chair.

The most important things to Mum are: her **job**, her **friends**, going **running**, **coffee** and most of all... **me**!

# This is Mel
## the diabetes mammoth

Mel has been living with us since I was 3.

Sometimes Mel's ok and I don't mind him, but sometimes he doesn't behave and then he's a **big** problem. Mel's a bit magic because he grows when my diabetes is being a problem.

The most important thing to Mel is: me taking care of my diabetes. He also likes juggling and plate spinning.

2

I need to check my
blood glucose and take
my insulin to look after
Mel and my diabetes.

Sometimes I forget to take insulin
when I have snacks and Mel doesn't like it
because my blood glucose goes really high.

Mel can be a total pain when it's hot and I'm trying to play football.

And sometimes Mel gets in the way
for no reason at all which is ...

## REALLY REALLY ANNOYING!

Mel gets really **big** when me
and mum argue about him.
I slam my door and
Mum shouts.

We both feel sad.

Me and Mum have got a mammoth problem. We need to shrink Mel and get him to behave again.

Very good at shrinking mammoths

First we went to see my diabetes team because they're good at helping us shrink Mel.

Then we went to play at my friend Aneesha's house. Aneesha lives with **Sid** the diabetes hedgehog so she *really* understands what it's like.

# Me and Mum have made a plan to shrink Mel

## My jobs

- Count to 10 instead of slamming the door

- Talk about my feelings with Mum and Mr Williams at school

- Practise my calm breathing when I'm cross

- Play football with Mum

- Draw a picture of how I feel

Signed: _Jake_

## Mum's jobs

- Talk to Jake about his day and not just Mel

- Talk about my feelings with Jake and with the support group

- Go for a run

- Play football with Jake

Signed: _Mum_

# We did it!

Mel is small again and we can manage him now.

He doesn't go away and I
still need to look after
him but that's ok
because he's part of me
and part of our family.

# Activities

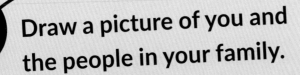

Draw a picture of you and the people in your family.

What is important to each of you?

**?** What super strengths and skills do you and the other people in your family have?

If your diabetes was a creature what would it be?

Draw a picture of your diabetes creature and give it a name.